Praise for *Living and Lovi*

M000229461

In his new timely book of poetry *Ice Sage: Living and Loving the Land* Levi Lyle has managed to touch us all, in the same and different ways. From *"My Dinner 'Tis of Thee"* to *"One Trip Farming"* he weaves a message of loss of jobs and the saving of soil into one unique tapestry. He recalls a past not so pure, a present not always perfect and a future to long for. This one book of poetry captures the essence of life on the prairie for an organic farmer from space to our own backyard.

Jeff Moyer, Fellow Farmer and CEO/Rodale Institute

Travel through life on an Iowa farm with Levi Lyle, as he serenades us with poems resembling a summer song of hope and renewal. From poignant reflections on nature's mysteries in the soil to careful criticism of our current food system, Levi transports you across time and seasons, urging us to pause and embrace the beauty around us.

Kathleen Delate, PhD. Extension Organic Specialist,
Iowa State University

Levi Lyle is an Iowa farmer and poet who cares deeply about being a good steward of the land and protecting the environment and about producing nutritious food on his farm. He beautifully expresses the need for regenerative, healthy soils as well as his concerns about "modern" industrial agriculture with its toxic pesticides, and the need to revive rural Iowa and America through his poems.

Ken Roseboro, Editor/Publisher *The Organic & Non-GMO Report/The Non-GMO Sourcebook*

Ice Sage

Living and Loving the Land Poems

Levi Lyle

ICE SAGE

Ice Sage: Living and Loving the Land Poems

Levi Lyle

Copyright ©2020 by Levi Lyle

First Edition.

Softcover ISBN: 978-1-4218-3665-2

Hardcover ISBN: 978-1-4218-3666-9

Library of Congress Control Number: 2020941063

All rights reserved. Printed in the United States of America. No part of this book may be used or reproduced in any manner whatsoever without written permission except in the case of brief quotations embodied in critical articles and reviews. For information contact:

1ST WORLD LIBRARY
PO Box 2211
Fairfield, Iowa 52556
www.1stworldpublishing.com

LEVI'S INDIGENOUS FRUIT ENTERPRISES
1045 210th St,
Keota, IA 52248
Aronialife@yahoo.com

About the Co-Publisher

Levi's Indigenous Fruit Enterprises was conceived for the purpose of coalescing forward thinking ideas about community under one umbrella. The common thread interconnecting all community relationships is reverent intentioned consciousness — ecological communities, human communities, and where they overlap (aka. our planetary community).

The use of the word "Indigenous," is intended to represent a balanced relationship with our planet — a symbiosis with Nature. The word "Fruit" is intended to refer to fruits-of-labor and a call to action.

If you value a vision for a more integrated and connected relationship with Earth, please share our works with others. Together we'll celebrate the communities we share.

About the Author

Levi Lyle grew up on a farm near Keota, Iowa, and graduated from the University of Northern Iowa with a BA in Science Education with an Environmental emphasis and a MAE in Post-Secondary Education. After ten years of teaching, counseling, and working as an academic advisor, Levi and his wife Jill returned to the farm where they raise their four children. Along with his interest in growing a variety of native fruits, Levi and his family grow and distribute fresh Aronia berries seasonally to local markets. Processing and marketing wild fruits is a passion that Levi feels brings balance to his other agricultural endeavors. Levi has worked as an organic inspector and now consults on the topic of organic transition. He has been a local leader in conservation no-till farming using roller crimping, a practice applied to cover crops that boosts sequestration on the prairie ecosystem – a role once filled by the buffalo in stampede. He passionately speaks about solving the global greenhouse gas dilemma by innovating Midwest farm policy to allow farmers to lead, which is the focus of the third book in this series.

Acknowledgments

Thank you to my parents, Trent and Joy Lyle, who taught me how to live and love.

I'd like to extend my gratitude to the following people and organizations: my mother Joy for editing, contributing poetic form to my ideas, and also for the cover art; my father Trent for supporting my ideas regarding agriculture and for contributing back cover art; James Galvin for support as the first reader of the manuscript; Guang Han for Chinese translations of two poems; and Practical Farmers of Iowa for their support and providing statistical information from the USDA.

Guang Han is an International graduate student pursuing a Ph.D co-majoring in Sustainable Agriculture and Agricultural Extension Education at Iowa State University.

For more information about Practical Farmers of Iowa, see their website practicalfarmers.org or give them a call 515-232-5661.

Thank you to the Iowa Poetry Association for first publishing the following poems in *Lyrical Iowa*: "Square Mile," "Lawn," "Prairie Ledger," "Seed Distributors (By Volume)," "Michael, the Tailor," "Loam" (originally titled Sod), "Green Manure (Cover Crops)," and "Prairie Volcanoes." Also, thank you to Iowa Telepoem for publishing my first audio recorded poems: "Square Mile," "Green Manure (Cover Crops)," and "KE TI WA (Meskwaki Indian word for Eagle)."

—Levi Lyle

"Winter under cultivation
Is as arable as Spring."

Emily Dickinson

Foreword

Iowa is a land formed by ice and fire. Change here took place gradually, over eons – until it suddenly accelerated. For thousands of years, glaciers covered the state, scouring slowly across the land. But as they melted, the places we know today as quiet streams were raging rivers, cutting tons of soil and rock from the landscape and hauling it downstream. Mudflats blew dirt for miles and stacked it up hundreds of feet deep, and hard ice and rock dredged holes in the ground, bequeathing marshy potholes that laced the land with wetlands and lakes. Geologically, the landscape was changed overnight. When the first people arrived in Iowa thousands of years ago, they saw a land of opportunity, and transformed raw material into a massive pastureland for grazing animal production, managed woodlands and farms around the edges. They wielded fire to encourage grass to grow, and sprawling oak savannas took root, nurturing interlinked communities of people and animals. Vast herds of bison thundered through the prairies, nourishing the soil and sustaining the people – and the haze of smoke hovering over the land, wafting the promise of green grass and the sustenance it signified, must have been a sight to behold.

When the first ploughs broke the prairie sod as the colonial pioneers sought land and opportunity in Iowa's fertile valleys, the pace of change quickened more. Railways followed and bison dwindled, while the first peoples and their nurturing fires were displaced. Over the last 75 years, the scale of change has been even more exponential. Dramatic transformations have succeeded one after another. Developments in technology, coupled with government policy encouraging research and specialization, have resulted in corn, soybean, hog, cattle, chicken and egg production numbers utterly unthinkable even as late as World War II. This tremendous output born of mechanization has not benefited everyone. While the number of farmers and the rural communities where they live has been in decline for decades, these losses have accelerated over the past 40 years, ushering in a cascade of unplanned consequences. As the farmers fled or sold out, the backbones of those rural communities – schools, churches, and small-town businesses – consolidated and shrank.

In the 1980s, that process reached a crisis point. Farms – and the rural institutions such as banks, hardware stores and even schools – were shuttering. Concerned Iowans formed Practical Farmers of Iowa to use science – on-farm research – to figure out farming solutions that kept profits, and soil, on their farms. PFI, like Iowa as a whole, has continued to rapidly evolve since its inception.

PFI's founding farmer, Dick Thompson, once said of the group: "We don't have all the answers, we're just trying to ask the right questions." That rings true today. We don't have all the answers, and the answers we do have are often different from those of our neighbors. But the curious, questioning farmers in our ranks are always asking new and bigger questions, never satisfied to stop searching for answers. PFI farmers are driven to seek – and somehow, however incompletely, find their own answers.

In this book of poetry, Levi embraces those questions with a whirlwind of visions. He takes us from the ice age to the future, to cultures around the world and back in time; from stunning beauty to moments of horror; from purple coneflowers to stop signs; from the eternal change of seasons to the work of wasps and bees. He recognizes the challenges, but his words bend towards hope. There is peace, for him, in the road to resilience – the clover, the earthworms, the dirt staying put, the rye pollen in the spring.

But more than anything, his visions force us to ask: Where did we come from? Where are we going? Where do we want to go?

As Levi wonders, "Where will we set off walkin' / beyond dreams by dawn / with our daughters on our backs?"

Nick Ohde
Practical Farmers of Iowa

Contents

Ice Sage

Living and Loving the Land Poems

Tone

The fitness of farmland:
epitaph in hieroglyph,
Venus of Milo in a grotto.

On shape, contour, slope, and grade,
productive crops condition
the stamina horses member.

Like a living organism's flagella
volitions her muscles,
field of winter cover crop wags

in a rain storm. Hell
or high water,
weather front upon weather front,

season upon season,
self contain a community;
rejoicing resiliency!

For ecosystems everywhere,
setting the tone.

Humus

Hues of borealis blue morning
glories between corn rows
seven species in awe
burst
in September sun —
days hauling harvest.

Without interseed, his workers (microbes)
take winter siesta,
pretend sleep to the naked. I
peer into the microscope
fully expecting to see
rations.

Bacteria unpack noguled roots,
feasted upon by cannibal nematodes — both predator and prey;
devoured by slugs and worms and impelled by
a mycorrhizal fungi hyphae —
the electromagnetic tide
spiders through the "life bread."

Seeing

My other eye
perceives a world
where throughput is reason
and real reason,
hard to come by,
is compost.
Rain showers and sunshine adorn
my skull, millennia since,
bleached white
half emerges
the rich black garden.
A peach stone germinated within
a sprout lifts through the socket
of the eternal one.

March Sheen

Not the equinox
nor first sign of spring
when imminent rains
stain into streams.

Not the gray reflection
overcast brings
nor the browns and reds
bled from virgin beds.

White shimmering moon;
breeze broad day light;
push and pull land
in high tide green sky.

The thought of it hiding there...
Just think, present all winter strong
beneath her slip—
cover crop.

Seed Distributors (by volume)

1. wind
2. water
3. bird, a dove or maybe a lark
4. mammal
5. Dow Chemical DuPont
6. BASF
7. Syngenta-ChemChina

Legacy of the Tortoise Afghan

The dense black loam of Mother Earth
is interwoven with the root tapestry of tall native grass —
a circuitry of neurons whose depths are her cortical brains.

A symphony of intelligence distinguishable by
diversity, reliance on community, and nature's selection
has become displaced by a noisy cloth tangle.

Underground annihilation of root, rhizome, and fungi;
retro cycles of water, carbon, and nitrogen;
besieged earthworms, emaciated small mammals, and monarchs
in silent want.

The Earth has become disjunct.
Man is but a ghost,
empty — treading on her shell.

Square Mile

One family, two families, three families, more
640, 320, 160 acres divided by four
steward oats, corn, soybean, hay and
rotate- the families multiply and stay.

Consolidate the farms
mechanize the man
increase the acres
mine what ye' can.

Progress
4, 3, 2, 1
close down the school
the kids have all gone.

《平方英里》

("Square Mile" translation by Guang Han)

一家、两家、三家，
有着六百四十，三百二十英亩土地，
四分成燕麦、玉米、大豆、牧草而轮作，
人们在这片土地上繁衍生息。

合并这些农场，
机械化那些农民，
夸大土地耕种面积，
尽你所能的开采自然吧。

预备，
四三二一，
学校解散，
孩子们从此离开了这片土地。

Morning Ritual

Before you naked, rising unhidden,
easy does the yoke roll alone in a purple bowl.
Centripetal we launch, sun and I flung,
gravity a ballroom step wherever day has begun.

Simple and the same but for fresh sweet blueberries,
nourishing, oats soaked in milk all the day carry.
Light of the day; at the dawn you are the map.
The tide… O, the tide… *hands folded in my lap*.

Footnote:

Inspired by a Walt Whitman poem titled, "O Captain! My Captain!."

Prairie Pastel

Tillage radish,
pulses, red
and crimson clovers fall
seeded.
Pounds and pounds
still hard rain
will not watercolor.

Omen of a Calling

Yellow jackets seize sweet
from fall strawberries ripe to eat.

"We exonerate no foragers!" angry wings lip.
Mine throb and well as I curse and spit.

From the ether of anger, from the ether of forgiveness,
arrives unfettered bittersweetness.

Nerves settle like a storm embraced,
sinuses pour down and pounding hearts race.

Through meridian channels ancient remedies sing —
poison of a wasp's sting.

Just then...,
healing.

Prairie Volcanoes

High noon volcanoes mushroom
in silhouettes breaking surf on wind.
Smolder silo stacks:
augered soybeans rain
down caldera vents.

Morning air is clean;
underneath tread, stubble crackle
too tough to harvest as noon nears;
stereo track of late September:
Fire throughout the Heartland.

Roaring white noise dubbing
all night. Fuzzy
soybean soot
from pots mixing —
combine.

God Love a Duck

In a starry sky, I see fires burning, and on the moon, day.
In November, the chill permeates the far side of Earth's stratosphere
as slivers of space dovetail down to us like fowl.
This is where winter comes

from. Smokish looking clouds
my nostrils exhort in
super cooled nebula.
Wood combusts into smoke
and so too does the water planet.
It is me you know, I am what I come from,
materially a state-of-transition.

The inhospitable Universe frosts our far side,
only good for keeping the human spirit humble;
out there, there are uncompromising grains,
therein lie — quantum mechanics, therein lie — ghostly probabilities.
God love a duck, from my lips
into the November above me and within.

Green Christmas

Heavy elements from super industrial smoke stacks,
leaping carbonized chains of carcinogenic soot
in strings of colored cereal
shackle the fir.

Earth hit so forcibly she leapt from prairie stores
to land
on green leaves;
the warming sphere detains flakes.

Forages Christ
to renew Earth
who thinks like ecosystems —
holy.

Pork Bellies

Sensational pleasure: Iowa State Fair
Pork chop on a stick.
Thousands of thousands
Pork bellies inseminate by plastic

Juicy and salty and savory
Tender and lean, no gravy
Pig you don't have to ask for
If you don't take it, sanctions collateral

Leave you with your civil war
Raise arms, where no farm, when we shut the door
Huts made from straw
Extremism crawl

Poke them, then smoke them
Right on the jaw.
Tomorrow's meek: the gristle
Turn the other cheek and come missile.

Footnote:
In this poem "crawl" is used as a noun to signify the conditions of
disparagement and hopelessness. In contrast, interpretation as a verb would
seem to imply reference to actions such as terrorism. The noun versus verb
dilemma is a metaphor for this cause-effect relationship.

Nine Zeros

The first land plant, Cooksonia, was a stem with no leaves.
The first fish did thrive within toxic pre-historic waters.

The first 3,000,000,000 years Earth characterized little diversity
While systems agreed to inner-rely.

The local teaches the universal:
Anti-biotic resistance about herbicide resistance;

Endocrine and ecology disruptors;
Monoculture gut flora and mass extinction;

Organ failure and agriculture nutrient runoff;
Undone, in my time, what eight more zeros took to build.

I see weeds in cornfields thriving without leaves.
I see fish in toxic waters.

I see fatty liver diabetes, cancer, gluten intolerance, and
  irritable bowels.
I see Multiple Sclerosis, Nuclear Palsy, and Fibromyalgia.

The news tells me megatons of heavy elements go up.
The way I am farming sends megatons of petro-chemicals down—

Tears streams and rivers up.
Tears stream like rivers down.

Michael, the Tailor

Spooler of futures;
seamster from the West

crossed Kingdoms without a map;
knit helixes to whirl open.

Snip code from The Artisan's threads.
Sew alive

Frankenstein.
Monsanto's thimble — people

without pattern
tailor of realms until pricked.

Rex Tillerson

Soil at least while it's there
defends its ground— even bare.
Spade the Earth
she'll still produce
but birds and bees will know the truth;
your heart has strayed,
entered the mistress
with your phallus cheap,
reaped a profit
when you went in deep.
Like oil and gold, all made for man, or so it serves to believe.
Our ego, our arrogance, our narcissistic petulance
lips "I love Earth, hurt it none, tiller' son."

Food Legacy

You had your chance
To do what's right
To prepare food
For our appetite.
But given the choice
Of what to include
Sucrose and fructose
You put in our food.

Now folks in masses
Have come around
Demanding food
More nutritionally sound
It makes me feel
like you don't care,
Feeding me food
From God knows where.

Prairie Stores

Walmart Corporation
Econo Foods Supermarket
Whole Foods
Good Earth Market
Keota Eagle Foods
New Pioneer Coop
Valley Natural Coop
Fareway
Dahl's
Sam's Club
Casey's General Store, Inc
Amish Country Store
Meskwaki Trading Post
Aldi
Six feet deep black silt —
incorporated B.C.

Stung

Coddled up in brain freeze,
another ice cold beer "to the bees."

A toast. On toast. If it's not yet out,
ration oil. Ration soil
as if flour for bread.

The flowers are female —
good in bed.

But they won't and better not;
nice girls not raised like that
or just all the bees are dead.

Sweet syrup from corn, beets, or cane
undo the natural world — a hurricane.

July all year
wasn't like this always —
a spoiled child with his toys.

The battleships and submarines;
the coast's reclaimed marines.

Jesus sees us
in fog and sorrow
ceases a good night's sleep —

starts work tomorrow.

Shot

Across the bough
Dew of open season
Parting sea of grass and fence and briar
Pastel blue lightning
Kick but nowhere to swim
Orange brims
Take whole horizons
Through smoking muscle
Only nerves bellied over
Passover
The smell of it on his breath

At Last Elyse

You have arrived.
Tell me my dear
about the trip;
from stars by atom,
to body by cells;
learn bicycle,
navigate straights,
cocoon and wing.

Rebirth

Holding the future.
Along her mountainous curves of flesh, rises temptation.
Arcing upon herself throughout time, self-subsistent.
Thou art father is gently stern.

Now her child is conscious.
Labor not four or two, but always multiplied
by one future, extrapolated from unity— ether widening still.
Sexing her (the act), is time standing still.

Intimacy private in contemplation, where
in a warm steeple twelve men sit on stone-
cold sky— unforgiving;
her womb since the age of antiquity.

Knee to knee in lotus they form a circumference.
Body heat patiently gives rise into an arched sphere
soon lending capacities of maximum threshold in vibrational
  synchronicity.
This awakened scene atop the world's highest peak looking out,
  looking in.

Drumhead Craftsmanship

It requires a great deal of effort,   emotional toil,
        to stretch cow-skin,   truth,
over an ill-measured Djembe,   consciousness.

The Bee Song

Sitting at a stop sign in a hurry
A little bee flew in without a worry
Landed on my hand and the steering wheel
Going buzz buzz buzz, his rhythm I could feel

The light turned green and I had to go
The little bee came along but he didn't know
And as we sped the bee took to fly
He hovered in the air, as the world passed by

In a moment it occurred how amazing
That the Earth holds us down, while circling
And before I thought more the bee had to run
Sucked out by the wind like the pull from our sun

So now when I'm driving and I'm hurrying
I stop to think twice about the world we're in
Cause we're all in the middle and the center relative
To the world and the people among whom we live

And as I'm standing on the earth, spinning around
The sun comes up and the moon goes down
But like Einstein said about the speed of light
If you're riding on a light beam, time stops.

Bury Me on the Prairie

When I die
Dig my grave shallow
In a field amid the lushest green clover.
Remove my boots
Remove my socks, for might
Surely their use isn't over.

I'll desire to know
I did good at heart
Didn't pollute, steal, or perpetuate greed.
And saw the big picture
Through eyes without tincture
Clear in my purpose and a life of good deeds.

Amid my loss you may mourn.
You may ponder my soul and feel wrench.
But so long you equally feel delight
That when spring clover
Blooms the sun over
Sweet nectar is visited by the finch.

Bury me out on the prairie
My resting place marked with coal
As cold as winter's white snow
And during the night
When all is dark
Those embers will light up my soul.

True love lives on
Outside of myself
In eyes that shine like yours
May the fire within
Those we leave as our kin
Come to know the parable of the sword (minor chord).

The cosmic prairie
Where we tred all our lives
Upon know where it is I've wound
Singing this tune
We'll reconvene
Before long becomes sometime soon.

"I long ago lost a hound, a bay horse, and a turtle-dove, and I am still on their trail. Many are the travelers concerning them, describing their tracks, and what calls they answered to. I have met one or two who have heard the hound, and the tramp of the horse, and even seen the dove disappear behind a cloud, and they seemed as anxious to recover them as if they had lost them themselves."

– Henry David Thoreau, *Walden*

Turtle Dove

A hound, a bay horse, and a turtle-dove
for them, I search the country far and above.
I walked the brooks by the night and day
but the people said "They did not come this way."

A hound, a bay horse, and a turtle-dove
I know they are out there disguised as love.
They wait for my return one day
where hounds have space and horses graze.

In pastures tall, and wide, and pure
a turtle-dove flies above the Earth.
One or two say they have heard the howl
or felt the trotting hooves rising through their bowels.

On the back of a spirited mare, perched a turtle dove.
Did you see her there? (rising in the clear)

Little Bird

Singing in the tree way up at the top
Little bird chirping is afraid he's gonna' drop
Summer days pass by now he sings a different song
My doubt is almost gone and my wings are getting strong
Fly fly away, fly away little bird
Fly fly away, fly away little bird

Take to the sky, sing another song
About the day you held the wind beneath your arms
Fly fly away, fly away little bird
Fly fly away, fly away little bird

Singing in the tree way up at the top
Little bird chirping is afraid he's gonna' drop
Fly fly away, fly away little bird
Fly fly away, fly away little bird

Summer days pass by now he sings a different song
My down is almost gone and my wings are getting strong
Fly fly away, fly away little bird
Fly fly away, fly away little bird

Take to the sky, sing another song
About the day you held the wind beneath your arms
Fly fly away, fly away little bird
Fly fly away, fly away little bird

Cornering a Possum

Eyelids
flutter
into marshal serenity
blows Mona Lisa's smile.
Vigilant
like the possum
corner
breath
so low
plum awed —
so subtly.

Almanac Moon Signs

Against our bodies
cornstand fell.
Rainforests of light,
ribbonwork in yellow kernels
sold. Out
on the family farm, flat
leaves belly
days, seasons, generations,
indicate the way— as do poles
on treeless prairie
stake heaven and point the way to travelers.

Lightning Thief

The longer I farm the more I find
I've got weeds of every kind.

Hit 'em with Roundup — chemical blast
At first they died but it did not last.

Hit 'em a second time at a double rate
Now food smells of glyphosate on my plate.

I'm sick of this poison, the bitter taste.
You can't beat nature at her own race.

Now I've a new set of tools: I'm the lightning thief.
Electric zap those weeds and cause them grief.

Gonna boil their guts from root to leaf.
Who knows, maybe we *will* save the coral reef.

Lawn

The prairie silently lives
harbored beneath small feet.
Timeless networks smile safe
from the plow's furrow,
glyphosate Roundup,
lime to alter pH,
tile to eliminate variability,
pesticide and fungicide,
on the side to "improve" agricultured soils.
Kids at play are shoelace seedsavers —
song birds that scatter wildflower germ.
Civilizations are weather to rhizomes
of big bluestem and rattlesnake master.
Still, Nature's Captain sounds,
"All small hands to the deck."

《草地》

("Lawn" translation by Guang Han)

草原静静地生长着，
庇护着下边的小脚，
永恒的网络在犁沟中安全地微笑。 (Timeless networks
smile safe)

农达草甘膦，
石灰来调PH值，
暗管排水去除了变化，
杀虫剂、杀菌剂在一旁，
"改善"着农业土壤。
玩耍的孩儿用鞋带系好自留种， (Kids at play are
shoelace seedsavers)

歌唱的鸟儿传播着野花的胚芽。
文明是响尾蛇的主人
和那经受风霜的大须芒草根茎。
自然队长仍然在召唤，
所有小手儿齐上阵。

Here Perennial

Purple coneflower
You hold the prairie with power
Even grazers great as the buffalo fail
To win the prairie where coneflowers pale.

Hive of honey bees
Government colonies
Fire and bear and ten million years
Chose a bee that would die for her peers.

Rivers drain the land
Cut through the rock to make sand
Loam untethered and skelter disdain
Here on the prairie where perennials reign.

Haiku

Berry harvest time
Inked purple fingers wash
Hark! School at last.

Organic Farmer

Smart as a whip and honest as Abe
she leaves no doubt,
while walking soybeans
amid clouds, bare roots swelter
on the canopy offering table.

Counts bushels in neighbors,
she helps weather farm recess-
ions in the soil. Attention,
intention and rotation pays.

Pod with wife and children,
volunteer kernels encircle ears.

To whispers in the mist
she yields.

Loam

Ten feet down holding on to what
ever can be wrap-strangle tied,
roots worm wander

Oceans stirred salty
particulates, seashells, and blue-green algae
to layer cake of sandstone

and bone. Broth washed
upon Iowa's shores, tide swelled, crest,
and broke upon beaches

The intercontinental sea between two mountains
Emptied — rivers drain in and rivers drain out
by way of loom

Triassic, Jurassic, and Mesozoic
spun to wheat, barley, and oat,
cake cooled

Wooly Mammoth play ground
to a halt,
frost slid away

Leafing sequesters,
chocolate frosting
this time

Green Manure (Cover Crops)

I dreamt I had wings
above autumn sky,
counted fields already breathing.

I dreamt like a race-streaked badger
I burrowed earth,
birthed soil.

I dreamt I was stolen
treasure,
a patched pirate buried.

Opened my one good eye
and found my wings
soiled.

The First Letter of Genesis

Envelopes the Sun mails
invisible first class parcels
deliver upon doorsteps,
a Norman Rockwell carrier.

Astronauts keep-
sake sentimentals of home
shuttle through far
beyond photon bundles transit

At, speeds light
toward this tiny Earth.
When clash of kindred spirits upon matter's mat
open white

letters in confetti.

Footnote:
The word "At" in this poem, used as both an adjective and preposition,
embodies the quantum paradox of light existing as both wave and particle
simultaneously and the impending significance.

Prairie Ledger

Bank-
prairie chicken
bobcat
spotted skunk
bear
zebra swallowtail butterfly
brown bat
river otter
sheepnose mussels
ornate box turtle
big and little bluestem
grasshopper mouse
aronia berry
purple martin
lynx
bald eagle
striped gopher
buffalo
gray wolf
mountain lion
-ruptcy

He Escapes to the Zone (that place of comfort)

Illusively he skirts,
darts, and improvises.
He is a foot "baller,"
a muscle bound ballerina.

Exquisite and alkali under pressure,
a centrifugal spin
on tip toes;
he pops a big gain.

Yearn, defensive foes
whose dance he knows;
fronts of four-two, four-three,
even eight men in the box.

No matter what they do
he just keeps running right on through —
with a burst of speed
the steed is freed, tucking that ball.

Stadiums of people
raised
with no fathers to speak of.

King Corn

How to imagine the toll:
In 2,400 years, land is stagnant bare but only 600.
Farms collect solar rays in fields of green canopy:
June, July, and August.
Imagine a brief four hour day rather than twelve.

Where light is stored:
Below, as well as, above ground;
Commerce for microbes and bugs
Barbeque pork sandwiches and grilled sweet corn with butter.

When corn grows,
Apostles Matthew, ~~Peter~~, Luke, and John,
If the other nine were gone.

Why 'not a blade or bug alive — in all
30 million acres in Iowa.

Haiku

Discomfort. Cold. Brief.
Ice baths do heart and mood good
Strength impacts others

Ice Sage

Helen once explained to me, 13,000 years ago an exploding comet impacted Earth near now Chicago with the power of thousands of megatons of TNT. This single event rained meteorites across the fire-engulfed continent sending up a thick layer of soot and dust that blocked out the sun for the next century. In a blink of geological time the charismatic large mammals like the wooly mammoth, giant sloth, and saber-toothed tigers were deleted; the ensuing freeze lasted 1,000 years.

Then, settlers arrived here to tear through the hewn roots that were so entwined only the single shovel bull-plow with a wooden moldboard and a team of draft horses could do the untethering. *My Granddad churned the ancient soil on this tract of prairie, turned it upside down so Earth's critters that resided in the sacred black silt could greet the mother-of-pearl sky. The afghan of bluegrass and hazel brush had been knit by Nature in the time since that catastrophic day.*

At Evening

Hide the gas can behind the tree;
if the women knew they'd raise a fuss.

We've got to get this fire lit
before the bugs kill us.

My Dinner 'Tis of Thee

You sold us food for our appetite.
That was your chance to fulfill what's right.
But instead of quality food, you plugged your brand.
Filled your pockets with cash in hand.

Pivot? Sure. To meet demand,
of course you are, because we forced your hand.
The stakes are tomorrow's children;
the stakes are, "Who owns control of land."

Now we must decide.
We must pledge.
We must awaken our consciousness
in farms we trust.

One Trip Farming

Could a' brewed whisky. Could a' fed his cows;
Could a' baled the straw to bed his sows.
But he left it in the field, rollercrimped rye down;
Doubled soybean profits earthworms abound.

Grow that biomass six feet high;
Memorial Day yellow pollen flies.
Rollercrimp upfront planting at the same time;
One trip farmin' is a friend of mine.

Down the Mississippi where the tributaries end
Clean waters flow for the fish to swim.
Pleasin' seein' coral reef abide;
The farm dirt's stayin' where God intended it reside.

Walkin'

Load all we love into our pack
Our daughters ride mounted upon my back
Far away, far away, until we're gone
Beyond dreams by dawn.

Tall grass, bluestem where we walk
Birds whistle, in silent solitude we can talk
On the path by sunrise
All is behind but what's before these eyes.

Travel. Journey. As seekers we embark
Walking through the valley of the shadow of the dark
My mind has wings, though the day looms large
I see your eye and it ignites my charge.

Lusty pines grow tall
Reminds me daily life is raw.
So I hold the image close, that all we love is in our pack
And I walk toward the horizon with our daughters on my back.

Midwest

Helen's eyes are the color of bailed and lofted hay
up in the barn for winter
where it will be fed or bed to livestock.

She is more frail with each passing season;
yet, daily writings root the unbounded light—
her soul from floating up even though it won't be long before
  wings.

KE TI WA

(Meskwaki Indian word for eagle)

A reeling bird lost between mountains
inundated with grief,
plowed by centrifuge into perpetual mourning,
periled by awareness of the impermanent self,
chemical reactions lift under charge
of electrical pulse

momentarily suspended between, leaping hitherto.

Long lasting are a sage's — who sits quiescent like a statue,
consciousness momentarily suspended as it is gone from telomeres.
Touching canyon walls leaped by neurochemicals.
Happiness to the sage looks all different;
trajections within mind are not indicative of emotion;
he may laugh or he may cry in this transient state of gratitude —
soaring without bearing between mountains.

Afterward

Iowans desire a legacy of healthy soils, healthy food, clean air, clean water, resilient farms, and vibrant communities. In reality, this seems idealistic. Iowa, by the day has ever fewer and bigger farms, less diversity, more inputs, poor water, soil loss, habitat loss, and dwindling rural schools and communities.

- In the last 55 years, the number of Iowa farms has decreased by nearly 75% —206,000 farms to just 89,000, while the acres farmed has remained steady.

- Iowa used to be a leading producer of oats, apples, potatoes, cherries, wheat, and more. Today, Iowa farms predominantly raise corn, soybeans, and hogs.

- Iowa is the nation's top pig producer. But profit per pig today is just over $6, a drastic decrease from the $111 per pig in 1976.

National Agricultural Statistics Service (NASS), USDA.

From 2010 to 2018, 69 of Iowa's 99 counties declined in population.

Des Moines Register, 2019

Iowa's water quality is getting worse, in part because Iowa's main crops leave the ground without living roots in the soil for about half the year. With no roots to bind up nutrients, they wind up in Iowa's surface waters and eventually, the Gulf of Mexico.

United States Environmental Protection Agency (EPA).

Iowa's predominantly two-crop system has increased farmers' dependence on costly inputs like synthetic fertilizers and pest and weed control products.

Economic Research Service (ERS), USDA.